Office Haiku

James Rogauskas

THOMAS DUNNE BOOKS / ST. MARTIN'S PRESS   NEW YORK

This book is dedicated to my parents.

THOMAS DUNNE BOOKS.
An imprint of St. Martin's Press.

OFFICE HAIKU: POEMS INSPIRED BY THE DAILY GRIND. Copyright ©
2006 by James Rogauskas. All rights reserved. Printed in the United
States of America. No part of this book may be used or reproduced
in any manner whatsoever without written permission except in the
case of brief quotations embodied in critical articles or reviews. For
information, address St. Martin's Press, 175 Fifth Avenue, New
York, N.Y. 10010.

www.stmartins.com

LIBRARY OF CONGRESS CATALOGING-IN-PUBLICATION DATA

Rogauskas. James.
   Office haiku: poems inspired by the daily grind / James
Rogauskas.—1st ed.
      p. cm.
   ISBN 0-312-35248-4
   EAN 978-0-312-35248-6
   1. Haiku, American.   2. Office politics—Poetry.   I. Title.
PS3618.O45O34 2006
811'.6—dc22

                                             2006040198

First Edition: June 2006

10 9 8 7 6 5 4 3 2 1

Contents

Introduction: You Too Can Haiku   I

Monday Mornings Suck   9

Kohi (Coffee)   18

No Sanctuary   24

Clock Watching   27

Existential Malaise   32

Work Flow   38

Lunch and Other Food   56

Chewing Gum   69

Office Politics/Coworkers Are Hell   72

Afternoon Boredom   9I

Departmental Meetings   95

Paper Cuts, Office Equipment,
   and Other Maladies   99

Anywhere but Here   108

Holidays and Such   114

Acknowledgments

Id like to thank my editor, John Parsley, at Thomas Dunne Books, and my agent, Ted Weinstein of Ted Weinstein Literary Management. I thank my wife, Arlynda Lee Boyer, for doing all of the work related to this enterprise that I didn't want to do, and I thank my sensei, John J. Jones Jr., for getting me hooked on haiku in the first place.

Introduction:
You Too Can Haiku

You too can haiku—
It's simply the syllables
All printed to fit.

First, five syllables
Line two—seven syllables
Five more, and you're done.

Why write haiku?

Haiku may be an ancient Japanese poetry form, but it's the perfect poetry form for a society conditioned to pay attention to nothing longer than a fifteen- or thirty-second commercial spot. With practice, you can *compose* a haiku in that amount of time.

Haiku also teaches mental discipline. With only seventeen syllables to express a thought or tell a joke, it trains a mind to cut a lot of fat out of its sentences. It keeps the mind nimble for selecting words and forming phrases; you not only have to convey your thoughts, but haiku forces you to pick and choose your words. The word you first select may have too many or too few syllables. The first word you think of that has the correct number of syllables may not have the precise shade of meaning you wish to convey.

I like to compose haiku for its own sake, but I also like to compose haiku when I'm pissed off at something. Instead of counting to ten, why not count to seventeen? Composing a haiku distracts you from your anger, allowing you to calm down.

Many annoying situations, when described in haiku form, sound like a Zen joke.

When used without care
The stapler pinches my hand.
I curse a blue streak.

Haiku can also be rather addictive, and although it's known among the Japanese that people become obsessed with haiku, one doesn't have to be Japanese in order for this to happen.

Haiku as verbal
Crack—I have a minimum
Five-a-day habit.

One of the great things about haiku is that it can be informal, particularly compared with the opinion most people have about "poetry." There is no room for bombast or lofty artistry if you're only using seventeen syllables.

Generally, the structure breaks down into five syllables on the first line, seven syllables on the second line, and five syllables on the last line. There are other formats you can use, but 5-7-5 is considered the standard.

Haiku does not have to rhyme. Rhyming is something of a hang-up with the English-speaking Western world. Not all Western poetry rhymes, either. If you want to include rhymes in haiku, feel free.

Some of my favorite haiku were written by Kobayashi Issa, a Japanese haiku master who lived from 1763 to 1827. Since he wrote in Japanese (and these translations are in English), the syllable structure in these haiku won't match the 5-7-5 pattern. These delightful translations are by Robert Hass.

> New Year's Day—
> Everything is in blossom!
> I feel about average.

Don't worry, spiders,
I keep house
Casually.

I'm going out,
Flies, so relax,
Make love.

Even with insects—
Some can sing,
Some can't.

Writing shit about new snow
For the rich
Is not art

   If a great Japanese haiku master can write about flies making love, why not write about a stapler, or the Super Bowl half-time show?

■ ■ ■

Haiku can be surprisingly easy to write, and they pop up in the most interesting places. On Interstate 64, not far from my house, there's a sign that says:

> When fog on mountain
> Be alert, and drive slowly
> Turn on lights

Put the word "your" before "lights," and change "lights" to "headlights," and it's a haiku.

> When fog on mountain
> Be alert, and drive slowly.
> Turn on your headlights.

The first line even sounds like something that might have been translated from Japanese.

Haiku is a very accessible poetry form. Because of its brevity, it's almost disposable; yet the simple act of reducing an idea to this form can make it profound.

It's easy to compose haiku. Just start out with a regular thought and hammer it into the proper number of syllables. With a very small amount of practice, you can see your compositions improve. You may even eventually find yourself obsessed with haiku, using it as a refuge from your own personal tormentors in your place of employment.

> My thoughts fall into
> Seventeen-syllable chunks;
> I am fortunate

> Haiku foster the
> Illusion that I'm doing
> Something real at work

I'm not a poet—
Just a disgruntled office
Worker with a pen.

Monday

Mornings

Suck

Barbaric, really—

Normally I would not be

Awake at this hour.

Definite whiff of

Pot smoke as I walk to work.

Are we in high school?

Had I known today

Would be this miserable

I would not have come.

Monday mornings—my

Sleepiness is at odds with

Pique at being here.

Sitting at my desk

As proudly as any serf

On his scrap of dirt.

I didn't shave for

Thirty-five K a year; I

Won't be shaving now.

Man, when I was small,

I always thought being an

Adult would be cool.

Jimi Hendrix say,

" 'Scuse me, while I vent my spleen!"

Were he office drone.

Kohi

(Coffee)

Dark, bitter, tarlike

You'd think it would kill someone

To start a fresh pot.

Jitters, coffee breath,

And frequent urination.

What more could I want?

Giving up coffee—

Irritability with

Some blinding headaches.

At my first "real" job

Cream was never put away.

Black with sugar, please.

Late afternoon cup—

The coffee is cold and stale.

Drink it anyway.

No

Sanctuary

Single occupant

Bathroom is locked. Why knock? Door

Didn't lock itself.

Why don't you remind

Me to page you the next time

You're using the can.

Clock

Watching

Ten-thirty seems so

Dreadfully early—half an

Hour later, not so.

In my cubicle

I sit; envying the dead

Two hours left to go.

The longest hour of

The week; is it Monday's first

Or Friday's last hour?

If it has to be

Friday, why couldn't it at

Least be five o'clock?

Existential

Malaise

If I could read minds,

I would certainly have a

Better job than this.

Wet blanket e-mail

Casts a pall over the rest

Of my afternoon.

Life is a burden;

This job but icing on my

Existential cake.

Dissatisfaction

Gnaws like a cancer in my

Troubled little mind.

My labors complete,

And I am left with the thought:

What was I thinking?

Work

Flow

Morning assignment.

Did you plan to wait 'til lunch

Before you told me?

You know—nobody's

Supposed to be here 'til nine . . .

Why is there work here?

While away sending

Your FAX, you continue to

Issue work for me.

Transcribed verbatim

As dictated. Yet, they still

Call it a "typo."

My whole life spent in

Preparation for this task—

What were you saying?

Priority job?

As were the last six that were

Supposed to be done.

If you want it fast

Maybe you should make sure that

Your part is done right.

Thank you for your rude

Interruption; you've destroyed

A quarter hour's work.

How to do nothing

Without looking like you are

Just doing nothing.

Sitting at my desk

Surfing surreptitiously.

Don't want to get caught.

Passive aggressive?

Maybe—but you're not getting

It any sooner.

I don't mind sharing

Work assignments—but you could

At least tell me first.

I can't type these if

You're going to hoard them and

Give me six at once.

Toll-free support line—

"Hold" music less annoying

On company time.

If it's so freaking

Important **now,** why'd you lose

It in the first place?

Would you do this—in

A cube, for some rube? Would you,

Could you, Sam I am?

Giving dictation

You could try spitting out the

Marbles from your mouth.

Lunch

and

Other Food

As slow as you all

Are, I could be back from lunch

By the time you leave.

People stultified

By the cafeteria

Menu—idiots.

Why read the damn sign?

In a dozen steps you'll **see**

What they have for lunch.

Overcooked, salty,

Boiled limp—lunch prepares you for

The rest of your day.

Cafeteria

Cabbage—always like it more

Than I think I should.

Pepper steak! Thou vile,

Traitorous dog—will I e'er

Be rid of thy burn?

Cafeteria

Pepper steak might be **made** from

Vile, traitorous dogs.

Potato crunch fish

Three words one doesn't expect

To describe one thing.

Taco day in the

Cafeteria—always

Yields the longest wait.

Old people shuffling

Precariously with food

Trays; rolling roadblocks.

A hush descends like

A spreading wave; someone has

Microwaved popcorn.

A bundt cake sitting

On a desk in an empty

Office—so tempting.

Chewing

Gum

Bored with chewing gum—

Really, how many kinds of

Mint flavor are there?

I wonder: what puts

The chevron pattern on a

Stick of gum, and why?

Office Politics/
Coworkers
Are Hell

Obstacles to your

Career—more staying power

Than Rasputin had.

Would Stalin have put

Up with this? No—he'd wipe out

Your entire village.

Office politics—

Being male, much easier

To feign ignorance.

The headline will read:

"Supervisor beaten to

Death with coffee mug."

I asked a simple

Question—I don't really want

Your whole life story.

Were you communing

With another dimension

While I explained it?

Why is it we're not

Still in trees flinging feces

At one another?

Office doublespeak

Gushes forth, an untamed spring.

Was that "yes" or "no"?

I did what you asked.

Of what you **meant** to ask for,

How should I know that?

The office snitch knows

More about your personal

e-mail use than you.

"This has to go out?"

And I was waiting for desk

Fairies to type it.

More I learn about

Coworkers, I find, the less

We have in common.

Supervisor comes

Around, vaguely muttering.

And leaves the same way.

I'm surrounded by

Freaking idiots and they're

Slowly closing in.

If you'd **read** my note

You would know the answers to

These stupid questions.

Hovering over

Me like a vulture; get the

Hell out of my cube!

All the bile in the

World, wasted on these soulless

Smiling backstabbers

At least in prison

You get to shank people who

Really annoy you.

Afternoon

Boredom

I sit wondering;

Can someone die of boredom?

Only time will tell.

Windowless office.

Some days it would even be

Nice to see the rain.

Pried my thumbnail off

With the staple remover

Just to stay awake.

Departmental

Meetings

Required attendance.

It was so much like high school—

Wanted to cut class.

Important meeting

My ass—you're just going to

Bore us for two hours.

Just like high school—sit

In the back of the room in

Case you fall asleep.

Paper Cuts,
Office Equipment,
and Other Maladies

The broken stapler—

Bear this soldier away from

The field of battle.

My pen fails to write;

Is the nib worn out, or is

It reluctant ink?

Chair adjusts six ways;

Who let Quasimodo sit

In my freaking chair?

Paper cuts might not

Always be from paper, but

They hurt just the same.

Real reason we're not

Chained to desks; health plan won't pay

For own limbs gnawed off.

No personal desks.

I have been here two years and

Still feel like a temp.

Knowledgeable staff

Has done this task for years—still,

Toner everywhere.

Rebooting desktop—

The more often it happens,

The longer it takes.

Anywhere

but

Here

Distracted by thought;

Where would I be, doing what?

If I wasn't here?

Anywhere but here;

I hear that Memphis is nice

At this time of year.

Would I prefer to

Be here, or have bamboo shoots

Thrust under my nails?

In Tokyo, it's

Already Friday night; god,

I wish I were there.

Would I rather be

Here, or running with the bulls

In Pamplona, Spain?

Holidays

and

Such

Fire alarm is called.

Unfortunately, the chance

Of fire is remote.

Back from vacation

So soon? We missed your take-charge

Style of management.

Company Christmas

Parties—passive aggression

Taken to new heights.

Wotan, Thor, Freya—

I think I like Saturn's day

The best of them all.

Today is payday—

For one brief, shining moment

It all seems worthwhile.